Original title:
Shadows in the Snow

Copyright © 2024 Creative Arts Management OÜ
All rights reserved.

Author: Arabella Whitmore
ISBN HARDBACK: 978-9916-94-602-2
ISBN PAPERBACK: 978-9916-94-603-9

Lurking Beneath the Surface

In the quiet of the night, they prance,
Little critters in a frosty dance.
Chasing tails, oh so sly,
Wondering why the snowflakes fly.

Snowballs bounce like crazy fools,
Fluffy hats on furry mules.
Every footstep hides a tale,
Who said winter's fun can't prevail?

Enchantment of the Frosty Veil

Jokes are told by frozen trees,
Whispers caught in winter's breeze.
Every flake a cheeky grin,
Catch them laughing as they spin.

Under blankets soft and white,
Squirrels giggle, what a sight!
Warming up by fireside glow,
The world's a stage for winter's show.

Enigmas Entangled in Snow

Strange footprints lead to places new,
What's a llama doing in a shoe?
Pine cones snicker as they land,
While rabbits plot to steal our hand.

Mittens missing from the line,
Petty theft? Oh, how divine!
Snowmen wink, their noses bright,
Who knew frost could spark delight?

The Frosted Layers of Time

Memories slip, oh so discreet,
As icicles dangle on trees so neat.
Bears in hibernation snore,
Dreaming loudly, winter's roar.

Time freezes in a goofy pose,
When playful winds start to doze.
Let the frosty fun unfold,
In this chill, be brave, be bold!

Illusions of Icicle Dreams

Tiny crystals dangle, bright and bold,
They take a dive when the warmth unfolds.
A slip, a slide, oops! Down they go,
Chasing my mittens in a frosty show.

Frosty fingers pinch my nose, oh my!
As I tumble in laughter, can't deny.
The trees start to giggle, the winds take flight,
"Keep your balance!" they tease, "or lose the fight!"

The Echo of White Stillness

Whispers of winter tickle my chin,
As snowflakes waltz, round and round they spin.
I trip on a snowdrift, laugh like a loon,
With a snowman grinning, let's dance to a tune.

A plump little bird, all bundled in fluff,
Looks at my face, says, "That's quite enough!"
I swish and I sway, with grace so defined,
But end up face-first, oh, poor me! Never mind!

The Veiled Horizon

The horizon blends like a painter's delight,
A landscape of munchies, oh what a sight!
With mittens for snacks, I munch and I crunch,
Beware of that snowman, he looks like a lunch!

I build a fine fortress, a castle of frost,
But the wind plays a prank, my kingdom is lost.
The grumpy old trees start to groan,
"Why can't you keep still? Can't you build on your own?"

Mystery in the Winter's Whisper

The ground speaks softly, a giggle or two,
As I slip on a patch, with a comical 'whoo!'
Noses all rosy, in the cold they shine,
I'm cracking up laughter; oh, life is divine!

A rabbit hops by, twirling with cheer,
His ears are all fluffed; he's the jester here.
We dance through the flakes, a hilarious pairs,
The world may be white, but humor declares!

Frost-Kissed Secrets

A snowman winks with pebble eyes,
As kids run past in winter's disguise.
A carrot nose that sprouted wide,
Conceals the giggles they can't hide.

A fluffy hat sits slightly askew,
Frankly wondering who wore it too.
With every tumble, a snowball flies,
Creating laughter beneath gray skies.

Silvery Forms Beneath the Drift

When flurries fall, the world turns bright,
Yet squirrels plot mischief, what a sight!
They burrow deep, then leap with flair,
Stealing nuts, unaware there's a bear.

Each footprint left tells tales of play,
Of snowball fights that made them sway.
With puffs of breath, they dash and dive,
In winter's game, they're all alive!

Glistening Shapes on a White Canvas

There lies a fort, proudly built,
With walls of snow, no trace of guilt.
The kids declare a glorious reign,
While one slips down, full of snow mane!

A sledding hill, an icy ride,
Where laughter echoes, who can hide?
From hilltop dreams, they tumble free,
Creating stories for all to see.

Echoes Beneath the Icy Veil

The breath of winter sings so clear,
As snowflakes dance, we all endear.
A puppy pounces, ears all aglow,
In pursuit of a snowball, oh, what a show!

Up in the trees, the branches creak,
Feeling the weight of winter's cheek.
Yet all prepare for the grand snow spree,
As laughter rings through each frosty glee.

Echoing Dreams in Celestial White

In a world of fluffy fluff,
Rabbits roam, oh so tough.
Snowflakes dance on frosty air,
Making snowmen with a flair.

Snowball fights break out with glee,
Chasing friends 'round every tree.
Giggling voices fill the night,
With icy jousts, a frosty sight.

The Luminous Veil of Frosted Night

Twinkling stars above us gleam,
As we build our winter dream.
Snowmen wear mismatched hats,
Silly scarves wrapped tight like spats.

Icicles dangle like bright bling,
While we laugh and dance and sing.
Our cheeks are red, our noses bright,
In this whimsical, frosty light.

Silent Footprints

Tiny prints on snowy ground,
Leading to the lost and found.
A cookie here, a cupcake there,
Whispers of a sweet affair.

Elves with snowballs, giggles too,
Writing messages just for you.
Every footprint seems to say,
Join us for some funky play!

Ghosts of Frost

Whispers haunt the chilly breeze,
Frosty giggles through the trees.
Bouncing snowflakes, dodging fate,
As winter's pranks tempt to create.

Skating on the pond's glassy sleeve,
Practicing to twirl and weave.
Frosty spirits cavort and play,
Chasing grown-ups on their way!

Whispers of Frosted Echoes

A squirrel on a treetop, so spry,
Wore a scarf that could make you cry.
He slipped on a branch, and oh what a sight,
Fell into the snow, what a frosty delight!

The penguins were dancing, quite a show,
In tuxedos, with style, they put on a glow.
They waddled and tumbled, quite filled with cheer,
Throwing snowballs and giggles, oh dear, oh dear!

Veils of Winter's Embrace

A snowman with buttons, two mismatched eyes,
Claimed to be ancient, with countless goodbyes.
He spoke of the warmth of the sun on his face,
But melted away with a hint of disgrace.

The rabbits were plotting a sneaky surprise,
Dressed in tight costumes, they caught winter's eyes.
They hopped through the drifts in a mischievous spree,
Leaving footprints that looked like a wild jubilee!

Silhouettes in a Winter's Hush

Two owls in a tree, of wisdom, they boast,
Spying on snowflakes, they'd gossip and toast.
They'd hoot about penguins and skiers galore,
While falling asleep, they'd knock on the floor.

A bear in a parka, so fluffy and round,
Stumbled on ice, making a thump with a bound.
He grumbled and mumbled, and got stuck in a drift,
As murmurs of laughter became quite a gift.

The Dance of Cold Remnants

A moose in the meadow, trying to dance,
With antlers that swung, it looked like a prance.
He tripped in a puddle, but laughed all the same,
Yelling, 'Winter's no time for the shy or the tame!'

The children were sledding, with glee in their eyes,
They raced down the hillside and covered in pies.
With splatters of whipped cream and laughter so bright,
Winter's the canvas for their frosted delight!

Secrets Caught in Haze

In the frost we tippy-toe,
Giggling where footsteps flow.
A snowman's hat has flown away,
It's stuck upon a deer's bouquet.

Snowflakes fall like clumsy sprites,
Landing on our noses bright.
We throw a ball, it hits a tree,
Laughter echoes, wild and free.

The snowball fight takes a twist,
A dog, now part, cannot resist.
He bounds in glee, a goofy show,
Chasing after flakes below.

Hiding secrets in each flake,
A world of giggles we awake.
Wandering through this frosty maze,
We uncover joy in winter's haze.

Glimmers of Dusk

At twilight, the world's aglow,
Icicles glimmer, a frosty show.
A rabbit hops with such great flair,
But slips and lands—oh what a scare!

The sun dips low, a comic scene,
Snowmen dance in winter's sheen.
They twirl around, all faces bright,
Until they fall in pure delight.

Doggos chase a snowball cheer,
While kids dive in, without a fear.
A giant skater's graceful spin,
Leads to a tumble and uproar within.

Laughter echoes with every gust,
In evening air, it's a merry thrust.
A little warmth in chilly air,
Glimmers of dusk without a care.

Pale Figures at Twilight

In the pale light, figures prance,
Strange forms in a frosty dance.
One's a snowman with a flailing hat,
Who can't seem to get used to that!

Skiing downhill, oh what a mess,
With tangled limbs and winter's dress.
We crash and laugh, a tangled heap,
The slopes now echo, joy runs deep.

A snow angel's wings they try to make,
But it turns into a frozen cake.
And then a cat jumps in the fray,
Leaving paw prints in our play.

So we cap off this twilight spree,
With mugs of cocoa, oh so free.
In frosty dusk, where giggles swell,
We find pure joy—who could tell?

Silhouettes in the Chill

In the evening, figures glide,
Chasing after dreams they hide.
A squirrel, perched on a snowy peak,
Dives right in with a playful squeak.

A winter chase, our laughter spreads,
Dodging ghosts that play in threads.
A snowball flies—it hits a fence,
In the chill, absurdity's intense.

Twilight brings a chill in the air,
Yet we move with joyful flair.
Each slip and slide, a silly dance,
We tumble down in pure expanse.

Underneath the twinkling stars,
We share in tales of who we are.
In silhouettes where laughter's bright,
We cherish winter's goofy night.

The Quiet Abode of Ice

In a land where chill winds blow,
A penguin slips, oh what a show!
Waddling with flair, quite the charmer,
Even with frost, he's a non-stopper.

Icicles dangle, pointy and bright,
A squirrel skates by in sheer delight.
He dreams of nuts, puffed with pride,
But gains some speed and takes a slide!

Snowmen grin, their noses of carrot,
But then a dog comes, eager to parrot.
He grabs a stick, makes off with glee,
What a ruckus in winter's spree!

Frosty air filled with children's shout,
As snowballs fly, and laughter's about.
The quiet abode, it starts to quake,
With giggles as the ice begins to break!

Echoing Footfalls

Footsteps crunch on a winter's road,
Each one echoes, a scurrying ode.
A cat sneaks past in a fluffy coat,
Trying to catch a rogue snowflake's float.

With each leap, a tumble begins,
As snowflakes dance like whirling twins.
The cat, now lost in the powdered white,
Wonders if he'll start a snowball fight!

Behind him, footprints, quite a trail,
Forming a map, a winter tale.
But who could have left such a spree?
The dog leaps forth, oh let it be!

Together they romp, in carefree bliss,
Through drifts and hollows, they'll never miss.
Echoing footfalls, a joyful chorus,
In this frosty playground, oh how glorious!

Trace of a Silvered Phantom

A ghost in the snow, it opts to glide,
With a floppy hat and no place to hide.
A ghostly bump, oh what a sight,
Trying to scare with frostbitten fright!

It wobbles and giggles, can't keep still,
While searching for snowflakes to fill its thrill.
It sneezes and snorts, a laugh to relive,
As children spot it, "Look, let's give!"

With cheeks made rosy, they shout with glee,
"Hey ghost, don't flee, come play with me!"
The phantom chuckles, floats in a spin,
As snowballs are thrown, let the games begin!

A trace of the phantom, frosted and free,
Turns into laughter, just wait and see.
In a frenzy of white, a winter's delight,
The ghost fades away, a magical flight!

Frosty Remnants of Light

In the morning, beneath the pale sun,
Twinkles of frost, oh what fun!
A reindeer leaping, oh so spry,
Slides on ice with a curious eye.

He spots a pile of snowball friends,
They gather 'round, the laughter never ends.
In their frosty enclave, they crack jokes,
About the winter's wildest folks.

Sunshine glimmers off icicles high,
As birds chirp tunes that seem to fly.
A laughing bear with a snow-covered nose,
Jumps in the fray, striking a pose!

Frosty remnants of sunshine's kiss,
Dance in the air, nothing amiss.
With giggles and cheers, the day unfolds,
In a world where laughter never grows old!

Frostbitten Memories

Once I slipped on icy ground,
The world spun round and round.
My sandwich flew, my hat went too,
All because of winter's view.

Those frosty tales come back to me,
Of chilly days and funny spree.
We laughed so hard, we lost our breath,
But enjoyed the frosty mess instead.

Lurking Shapes in the Silence

Behind the trees, a figure looms,
Could it be a snowman that zooms?
Or just a cat with frosty fur,
Deciding if it's time to purr.

We tiptoe close, with giggles near,
To find a creature – or a beer.
But in that moment, we just fall,
On the ice, the winter calls!

Ethereal Figures on a Chilled Path

Footprints lead into the white,
Maybe gnomes took off in flight?
Or generous elves that love to play,
In the cold light of a winter day.

We chase the paths with childish glee,
Tripping over snow, oh, can't you see?
That laughter echoes, high and clear,
As snowflakes dance – the end is near!

The Quiet Imprint of Winter's Breath

Whispers float on frosty air,
Chasing rabbits without a care.
But there, in snow, what do we find?
A donut-shaped snowman, blind!

He rolls and tumbles, oh so spry,
With each big bounce, we can't deny.
Those frosty frolics, oh what a show,
In our winter wonder, we steal the glow.

Mists of a Frosty Dusk

In a winter wonder, we trudge and we slide,
Snowballs a-flying, our giggles can't hide.
A snowman that wobbles, with a carrot for nose,
He suddenly topples, as everyone knows.

With scarves wrapped tight, and earmuffs askew,
We build icy towers, what a sight to view!
Wait, is that a penguin or just a friend?
Oh no, it's just Phil, on that box he'll descend!

Puffed jackets in colors that clash and collide,
Making snow angels, with arms stretched wide.
From snowball fights fierce, to snow forts so grand,
Our laughter takes flight, like a snow flurry's band.

At dusk, we all gather, sipping hot cocoa,
Thinking of snowflakes and their unique show.
But as we chat loud, the mug slips away,
Turns out the floor's slippery—a price we will pay!

Murmurs of Light in the Cold

Twilight whispers, as the day bids goodbye,
Footprints in the powder, beneath a gray sky.
An owl hoots softly, while snowflakes descend,
A snowball fight fuels mischief among friends.

With cheeks all aglow, and noses turned red,
We fumble and tumble, like bears seeking bread.
My mittens are soggy, my boots filled with snow,
But oh, the sweet laughter, it just steals the show!

Dancing in circles, we spin and we sway,
Each slip on the ice makes a comical display.
A tumble, a stumble, we land in a heap,
Snowflakes are falling, and so are our leaps!

Hot chocolate awaits, with marshmallows afloat,
We'll trade in our hats for a warm fuzzy coat.
The murmurs of giggles echo through the night,
In this frozen wonderland, everything feels right.

Traces of Light in Frozen Realms

Under moonlit sky, in the crisp, snowy air,
We race after snowflakes, without a single care.
Each puff of powder that dances in flight,
Like sparkles of laughter, against the pale light.

Now Phil's rolling fast in a barrel of fun,
His cheerful high-pitched squeak, second to none.
But a wobbly sledge, nearly sends him ahead,
Oops! He's in the snow, with a face full of bread!

Giggles erupt as we dart to and fro,
Leaving behind us trails of giggles and glow.
A snowball's a threat, but laughter's the aim,
In this crisp silver world, it's all just a game.

Amid all the frolic, let's ponder this night,
As we warm up together, till morning's first light.
We'll cherish the moments, the laughter we crave,
In this wintery haven, our hearts they will save.

Icy Phantoms in a Wintry Landscape

With each step we take, through the glittering frost,
Silly prancing about, not a moment is lost.
A penguin appears! Oh wait, it's just Dan,
With his arms flapping wildly, a homemade plan!

Snowflakes are spinning, a whimsical dance,
We twirl and we tumble, just taking our chance.
Sledding down hills, giggling trails we'll trace,
But careful, dear friend, don't run into my face!

The frozen wind whispers a cheerful refrain,
While we dodge icicles, and play in the lane.
In this icy expanse, we sculpt our delight,
Every grin sparkling, in the soft twilight.

As night draws us closer around fireside cheer,
We swap outlandish tales with a mug of warm beer.
The icy phantoms vanish, as dreams take their toll,
In these wintery realms, we've truly found our soul.

Snowbound Apparitions

Fluffy figures dance in white,
With snowmen sporting hats so bright.
A snowball fight, a playful spree,
Who knew frosty friends could be so free?

Laughter echoes in the chill,
While snowflakes land with grace and thrill.
The frosty air, a jolly tease,
Our frozen giggles bring us ease.

A rabbit hops, with leaps so grand,
Leaving tiny prints, a snowy brand.
Ghostly giggles fill the air,
As winter's tricks are everywhere!

Beneath the moon, we play and prance,
With frosty creatures in a dance.
Their icy mirth, a winter's jest,
In our frozen play, we find our best.

Glistening Eidolon

In a glisten, bright and bold,
A spirit leaps, or so I'm told.
With snowflakes stuck upon its nose,
It tumbles round, while laughter flows.

Icicles hang like teeth of glee,
A frosty grin for all to see.
We try to catch that twirling wight,
But all we grasp is pure delight.

A snowball flies, a playful fling,
As winter winds begin to sing.
With giggles loud and cheeks aglow,
What a splendid, silly show!

Through enchanted flakes, they flit away,
Those merry beings with icy play.
We'll chase them down till day is done,
And join their fun, oh what a run!

The Unheard Heartbeat of Winter

Inside the cold, a secret waits,
With silent beats behind frosty gates.
A heart that thumps in winter's throne,
Yet laughs from depths we've never known.

With mittens on, we stomp and glide,
While clumsy feet take every stride.
The frozen world gives a low cheer,
As giggles echo far and near.

Snowflakes whisper tales at night,
In frosty moon's soft silver light.
They plot mischief, so carefree,
As we chase dreams, so wild and free.

A lonely heart echoes 'cause,
Winter hides behind a fuzzy facade.
But oh, the joy found here and there,
In frozen realms, we shed our care!

Enigmas of the Winter Realm

In the snowy haze, a riddle dwells,
With fluffy tales that laughter tells.
A penguin slips on ice so slick,
Chasing giggles, oh what a trick!

Footprints lead to places bold,
Where frosty creatures break the mold.
A snow sage nods with a twinkling eye,
While winter whispers, 'Oh my, my!'

A flurry here, a swirl so bright,
Turns silent nights into pure delight.
We toss about in frosty cheer,
As mysteries bloom, our joy sincere.

With every snowball launched with care,
We build new worlds beyond compare.
For in winter's glee, we find our name,
In this riddle, we play the game.

The Weight of A Winter Ghost

In the crisp air, I trip on a toe,
My winter coat weighs more than a crow.
Snowflakes chuckle with each little fall,
As I waddle like a penguin - oh, what a sprawl!

A snowman grins, his eyes made of coal,
And I'm trying to regain my control.
But he's just a pile of frost and cheer,
While I dance around in my snowy veneer!

With every step, a crunch echoes loud,
I feel like the clumsy member of a crowd.
The ghost of winter is having her fun,
She's laughing at me, and I can't outrun!

So here I sit, on a pile of white,
The weight of my blunders just feels so right.
A snowy reminder to take it slow,
While the winter ghost continues her show!

Frost's Forgotten Secrets

The world wears a blanket, soft and bright,
Inside, I ponder, with a sip of delight.
What secrets does winter whisper and speak?
Perhaps my hot cocoa is feeling a tweak!

I stumble on ice, do a twisty ballet,
And the hot chocolate giggles, 'Drink me today!'
Marshmallows float like adorable fluff,
But they too are sly, 'Is that frosty enough?'

Snowflakes debate how to land on my nose,
Each one with a story that nobody knows.
Frosty giggles echo with sounds of pure glee,
As I squee through the snow, like a child, so free.

Oh, secrets of frost, you tickle and tease,
With laughter and mischief blowing through the breeze.
I'll chase every snowball that rolls down the street,
For winter's a prankster, and I can't be beat!

The Stillness Between Steps

In the stillness, I pause, then I slip,
Right on my bottom - oh what a trip!
The world holds its breath, it's a magical scene,
While I laugh at the mischief that's lurking unseen.

Each step I take feels like walking on cream,
And I think of a snowman who's living the dream.
Snowflakes perform in their own little show,
While I stand there, wondering where I should go.

There's a dance in the chill, awkward and loud,
While the trees all giggle, oh they're really quite proud.
In the quiet of winter, I find it absurd,
That the snow is the only one not feeling perturbed.

The stillness between offers a chance to chuckle,
At the slip and slide, as snowflakes huddle.
With smiles all around, I'm bound to embrace,
The joy of the season and its clumsy grace!

Misty Shapes in the Moonbeam

Misty shapes dance, in the sprite of the night,
They wear frosty capes, all shimmering bright.
I step on the ice, and I'm suddenly free,
Till I land with a thud—who knew it was me?

The moonbeams are laughing, what a curious sight,
As I try to juggle my chocolate delight.
They say, 'Welcome, dear friend, to our wintery ball!'
I guess frosty slips are the best kind of fall!

A snowflake approaches, with a wink and a spin,
"Would you like to join us, or should I just win?"
I nod with a grin, but I'm in quite a mess,
For my dance moves are silly, and I make quite a guess!

So here's to the mist, the moonlight, and cheer,
And the clumsy little antics of winter so dear.
With laughter all around, we twirl and we sway,
In the soft winter night, where giggles hold sway!

Ghosts of the Frozen Ground

In the stillness of the night,
I heard a sneeze and a fright!
A ghost in boots, oh what a sight,
Slipped on ice and took flight.

With giggles and howls, they're on parade,
Dancing in snow, unafraid.
The frozen ground is their charade,
Making snowmen that won't fade.

Laughter echoes through the chill,
As they slide down a snowy hill.
A whisper of mischief, a playful thrill,
Who knew ghosts had such skill!

In this winter wonder, we all partake,
The silly games the spirits make.
With every jig and jolly shake,
I'm sure they'd join us for cake!

Moonlit Figures in the Snowfall

Beneath the moon, they twist and twirl,
A motley crew of winter whirl.
Mice with hats, and cats that hurl,
Snowflakes dance in a frosty swirl.

Each flake whispers tales of fun,
Of silly races just begun.
A penguin slips, the laughter's spun,
As cold cheeks warm in night's run.

The rabbits wear their snowflake boots,
Dashing in and out like hoots.
Cartwheeling past with little toots,
Who knew snow could make such roots!

Under stars that shine like bells,
These figures frolic, casting spells.
With snowball fights and laughter swells,
Who knew winter could have such yells!

Hushed Footprints in Crystal Light

A crunching sound beneath my feet,
Leads to footprints quite a feat.
A duck in boots, oh what a treat,
Chasing snowflakes 'round the street.

In crystal light they softly glide,
Bunnies bounce, and kittens slide.
With fur coats warm, they can't hide,
From the antics of winter's pride.

Polar bears in top hats roam,
In this chilly, frosty home.
Making snow forts like they own,
In frosted fun, they're never alone.

With each step, they twirl and laugh,
Creating memories on their path.
In this cold, there's joy by half,
As winter's fun becomes the craft!

The Muffled Specters of Winter

In the depth of dusk, they whisper low,
Specters roll on the drifting snow.
With scarves and hats, they steal the show,
In puffs of laughter, they come and go.

A winter breeze brings hearty cheer,
While jolly sprites appear near.
With pranks and jokes, their intentions clear,
Come spin with joy; let's persevere!

Through fluffy mounds, they leap and bound,
In snowball duels, the fun is found.
With cheer and giggles all around,
Who knew winter would be this profound?

So if you hear a giggle's trace,
Know it's spirits in a playful race.
With every flake, they bring their grace,
In this frosty, whimsical place!

Translucent Veils on a Wintry Day

Waltzing flakes with giddy glee,
Chase the squirrels, oh look at me!
Bouncing boots with slushy sounds,
Slipping here and tumbling 'round.

Laughter echoes through the chill,
Winter's game, it's quite the thrill!
Snowmen sporting silly hats,
Waving at the giddy cats.

Giggles float on frosty air,
As penguins prance without a care.
Hot cocoa spills in merry fights,
Frosty noses, dazzling sights!

With a toss of flakes so bright,
We dance together, pure delight!
In this winter, laughter flows,
Underneath the drifting snows.

Elusive Dreams in a Snowbound World

A snowball flies and hits a tree,
Oh, what fun to laugh and flee!
Chasing dreams like drifting breeze,
Where snowflakes tease with little ease.

Mittens lost in winter's rush,
Snowman's eyes, oh what a hush!
Buttons missing, carrot gone,
Oops, hit the ground, fall like dawn!

Ice skating on a pond so slick,
Twirl and spin, what a trick!
Falling faces, giggles paint,
Every tumble, pure complaint!

Snow forts built with giggly bands,
While snowmen think they're rock bands.
Every flake a funny jest,
In this world, we're all the best!

The Pale Dance of Winter's Spirits

Wandering shapes in moonlit glow,
Laughing softly as they flow.
Twinkling lights dance overhead,
With every stride, the laughter spread.

With every puff of frosty breath,
Giggling ghosts of playful heft.
Skiing squirrels with tiny hats,
Chasing dreams from room to mats.

Whispers of ice in mischievous cheer,
Frolicking frostlings drawing near.
Cups of cocoa, stories told,
In winter's grasp, we bravely bold.

The night is nipped with cheer so bright,
Winter's spirits weave their light.
In every laugh and snowflake spun,
We dance until the day is done!

Beneath the Surface of Glittering White

Underneath the fluffy ice,
Bouncing bunnies, oh so nice!
Snowball battles in full swing,
With silly hats, let laughter ring!

Noses bright and cheeks aglow,
Frolicking through this chilly show.
Puppy prancing, tongues a-flap,
Dancing 'round a winter map.

Giggling kids in jackets tight,
Make believe in pure delight.
Giggles drift in snowy air,
As snowflakes catch a playful snare.

Up above the rooftops shine,
Whirling sparks that twist and twine.
Winter's mirth like dreams take flight,
In this dance of cold, so bright!

The Unseen Wanderers

In the quiet, something creeps,
With a giggle, through the heaps.
Snowflakes tumble, wearing hats,
As they play with furry sprats.

The trees wear coats, so big and wide,
They hide the squirrels from the slide.
A tumble here, a slide up there,
Snowmen grinning, unaware of flair.

Bunnies bounce with tails of fluff,
Hopping through their fluffy stuff.
With each leap, they make a scene,
A frolic on a canvas clean.

As day fades and laughter springs,
A touch of magic winter brings.
The unseen giggling all around,
In the icy playground, joy is found.

Dancers in the Flurry

In the swirl of winter's dance,
Chubby cheeks in a frosty trance.
A snowman twirls, a carrot nose,
As little feet stomp where he goes.

Flakes do the cha-cha, quick and spry,
While sleds race past, oh my, oh my!
Gusts whirling like a merry band,
Chasing snowflakes across the land.

Bears in scarves, a sight so rare,
Twist and turn without a care.
With frosted hats that flop and sway,
They jiggle and giggle, all the way.

Under the moon, the fun won't fade,
In this chilly masquerade.
With laughter echoing through the night,
The dance goes on in pure delight.

Hidden Shapes Amidst the Chill

Under layers of glittering white,
Little creatures peek from sight.
Round the corner, a snowball flies,
With squeaky laughter and surprise!

Paws leave prints like clumsy feet,
As they scurry, oh what a feat!
Dancing quietly in their game,
No two prints look quite the same.

A fluffle of rabbits, hopping about,
Making angels and giggling out.
The hedgehogs roll in a snowy embrace,
As winter's chill brings a giggly race.

Hidden shapes in an icy scene,
Winter mischief, oh so keen!
With laughter bubbling in the air,
Joy and snowflakes everywhere!

Impressions of a Silent Night

In the stillness, a rustle heard,
A snowball fight? Or just a bird?
Footsteps crunch on a frosty stage,
Whispers of fun at winter's age.

The moon peeks down, a wink or two,
Watching the wonder, frosty and new.
A towering snowman tips his hat,
As time wobbles and creatures chat.

A group of squirrels with acorn treats,
Holding a feast where laughter meets.
With every nibble, they share a tale,
Of winter frolic and joyful trails.

As midnight sirens softly chime,
The night is wrapped in playful rhyme.
Echoes dance, as stars ignite,
In the hush of winter's night.

Chilling Silhouettes

In the winter's frosty glow,
Figures dance with smiles aglow.
Snowballs fly, a playful fight,
Frozen giggles fill the night.

Snowmen wobble, hats askew,
They sneak a grin, and then they moo!
With carrot noses, quite absurd,
They plot a dance, oh what a word!

Sleds go zooming down the hill,
With squeals and laughter, voices thrill.
Frosty friends in swirling flight,
Chilling antics, pure delight.

Under stars, they prance with glee,
Winter whimsy, wild and free.
Not a grump in sight tonight,
Just frosty fun, hearts alight.

Haunting by Moonlight

Beneath the moon, a silly sight,
Dancing ghouls in snow so bright.
With floppy hats and mismatched gear,
They trip and tumble, bring the cheer.

Cold winds whisper secrets here,
While snowmen crack up without fear.
Ghosts of winter, full of flair,
In the dark, they slice the air.

They throw snowballs, make a mess,
All in fun, it's no distress.
With icy stares and playful fright,
These moonlit pranks keep spirits light.

Laughter echoes, mingles clear,
Frosty flights, no need to steer.
Under stars that glow so bold,
The funny hauntings, stories told.

Veiled Figures in the Winter Light

Mysterious shapes in snow draped bright,
Lurking softly, what a sight!
Are they friendly, vile, or shy?
With winter's laugh, they skip and fly.

Cloaked in white, the figures sway,
With little jigs, they laugh and play.
UFOs of ice, in tow,
They wiggle dots, and wild winds blow.

They peek from trees with cheeky grins,
Throwing snowballs, grinning sins.
Like tipsy elves in frosty cheer,
They whirl around with raucous jeer.

The night grows cold, but spirits heat,
With antics that are hard to beat.
Veiled in fun, the world so bright,
Figures dance till morning light.

Footprints in Frozen Laughter

Along the path, a trail of glee,
Left by friends and laughter's spree.
With each step, a chuckle shared,
In frozen realms, not one is scared.

With silly walks, they leave their mark,
Blending fun in the snowy park.
Giggles echo, footsteps prance,
In playful steps, they caper, dance.

Snowflakes land on noses bright,
Tickling cheeks, what a sight!
Frosty paths of joy displayed,
Leading home, where laughter's made.

As twilight falls, the prints remain,
In winter's game, there's no disdain.
With spirits high, the world now glows,
In frozen laughter, love just grows.

Shadows of a Frosted Dream

A penguin slipped upon the ice,
His flippers flail, oh what a price!
He wobbles like a jelly bean,
In a winter wonderland, he's the kingpin.

Bunnies bounce with snowflakes bright,
Hopping high, what a funny sight!
They get lost in marshmallow fluff,
Squeaking 'Help!' and 'This is tough!'

A snowman sneezed — what a shock!
His carrot nose took flight, a rock!
Down the hill, it rolled so fast,
He can't catch it; it's gone at last!

The snowball fights are pure delight,
But watch your back, it's a snowball night!
As laughter fills the frosty air,
Winter's fun is everywhere!

Eclipsed by Winter's Charm

A squirrel donned a woolly cap,
With acorns hidden in his lap.
He twirled around like he could fly,
But fell in love with a snowflake pie.

Two kids build a fort of ice,
Laughing hard, they roll the dice.
Snowballs fly, a friendly brawl,
And someone yells, 'Hey! Heads up! Y'all!'

A dog chased his tail in fray,
Sprinting fast, he made a stray.
He stumbled onto a pillow soft,
And rolled away, not dainty, but oft!

Ho ho ho, the winter cheer,
In cozy hats and grins so clear.
Each chilly breath, a frosty puff,
In this cold world, we can't get enough!

Frost-Covered Secrets

The snowflakes danced in merry glee,
As a turtle tried to dance with me.
His tiny feet slipped on the ground,
He twirled around, his shell unbound.

A rabbit's wiggle brought a grin,
With carrots tucked beneath his chin.
He hiccupped loud, oh what a sight,
As snowballs flew, adding to the fright!

A snowflake slipped and lost its place,
A tumble here, a funny face.
Through every twist, each snowy bend,
Laughter rang out, on it we depend!

The frosty world ignites our play,
Every stumble makes our day.
With chilly cheer that warms the heart,
In winter's grasp, we're all a part!

Echoes of a Winter's Glimpse

A cat in boots, he'll stalk his prey,
But slips on ice and shouts 'Oh, hey!'
With style, he falls—a fluffy heap,
While nearby kids at giggles creep.

The snowman wore a hat too big,
He tiptoed like a chilly twig.
But when the wind blew in so sly,
His hat flew off — a snowy spy!

The birds all chirp and share a laugh,
At the sight of a frozen giraffe.
He stands so tall in winter's pride,
But under snow, his humor hides.

Each laugh echoes in frosty air,
With winter fun, we haven't a care.
As giggles ring and spirits rise,
In this snowy world, the fun never dies!

Lurkers Beneath the Drift

In the snow, the gnomes play,
Making snowballs all day.
With grins as wide as the moon,
They'll strike with a friendly tune.

From underneath the pile,
They wait and joke for a while.
One pops out with a squeak,
A snowball fight makes them weak!

They tiptoe in fluffy boots,
Hiding behind frozen roots.
They giggle, but then they flee,
As a snowman shouts, "Catch me!"

With laughter etched in the frost,
These tiny pranksters are the boss.
So if you hear splashing sounds,
It's just gnomes having snowball rounds.

Pale Imprints in the Ice

Footprints dance like a jig,
Squirrels prance, it's all so big.
They scamper without a care,
While rabbits hide, a bit scared.

The deer glide like they're on skates,
Twisting 'round their frosty fates.
They slip, they tumble, then they laugh,
It's a comedy in nature's path.

A penguin waddles, quite a sight,
Stumbles and flaps with delight.
Each splash, a chuckle in the cold,
Nature's jesters, brave and bold.

The ice reflects their silly game,
As they prance without any shame.
In this winter wonderland so nice,
Life unfolds in frozen slice.

Ethereal Forms in Frost

Glimmers and winks, oh what a tease,
As frosty shapes dance in the breeze.
A ghostly figure skips so spry,
With fluffy mittens, oh my, oh my!

They swirl like snowflakes, round and round,
In a merry-go with no solid ground.
Then one slips on a patch of ice,
Frosty giggles, oh that's too nice!

With snowballs made of icy fluff,
They claim to be tough, but it's just bluff.
A frosty face, a gleeful grin,
Each playful spark, where chaos can win!

They twirl and spin, give it their best,
In a winter's madcap jest.
When the night falls and moonlight beams,
Frosty forms are funnier than dreams.

Spirits of the Storm

Whispers from the swirling flakes,
Dance with laughter, oh, what fun makes!
Spirits of snow with sprightly schemes,
Concocting mischief, wild as dreams.

They throw snow around with glee,
A flurry of fun, oh can't you see?
Each gust of wind, a joyful shout,
While snowmen wobble, and then fall out!

In the storm's embrace, they twirl and glide,
With playful grins, they won't subside.
They chase each other, tangle and trip,
In the snowy madness, they let it rip!

So if you hear a soft, silly cheer,
It's the spirits of winter, drawing near.
Join the laughter, let your heart soar,
In the frosty fun, forevermore!

Hidden Designs of Frost

In the morning light, oh so bright,
Funny shapes dance, a charming sight.
A snowman grins with a carrot nose,
Next to a cat in a frosty pose.

There's a penguin sipping a warm drink,
A polar bear in shades, what do you think?
The icy canvas draws laughter anew,
As winter whispers secrets in blue.

Elves with snowballs are having a blast,
With giggles and mischief, they're built to last.
Frosty laughter fills the chilly air,
In this world of whimsy, joy's everywhere.

Every flake tells a tale of delight,
Crafting moments that warm hearts at night.
So grab your mittens, come join the spree,
In this winter wonderland, wild and free.

Hazy Figures Amidst the White

Wandering figures blur in the storm,
Is that a dog, or a snowball swarm?
A bunny hops with style and flair,
Wearing a tiny, knitted hat with care.

A troupe of kids in a playful race,
Slide on sledge, oh what a chase!
Their laughter echoes through the pale glow,
As they tumble and roll in the sparkling snow.

Uncle Fred's lost and dressed like a bear,
With frosty whiskers way beyond compare.
Chasing a snowflake that danced away,
What a sight, on this frosty day!

Yet in the blizzard, we find delight,
With whimsical forms in the soft twilight.
Every turn brings a giggle, it's true,
A winter spectacle, just for you!

Glimmers of a Winter's Tale

A flash of sparkle, a dash of fun,
Under the moon, the games have begun.
Snowflakes twirl like little dancers,
Creating magic and wild prancers.

A group of gnomes with candy canes,
Conduct the snow, like musical trains.
They twirl and spin in winter's embrace,
Painting the landscape with frosty grace.

A frosty wizard lost in the fray,
Turned his familiar into a sleigh!
Around the trees, it zooms and flies,
Causing laughter and sweet surprise.

Every corner holds a playful scene,
In this winter's tale, where joy's routine.
So grab a friend and join the cheer,
For the magic of winter is drawing near!

Whispered Memories in the Cold

Frosty whispers float on the breeze,
They tickle noses, and just tease.
An icicle's jingle, a joyful chime,
In this chilly world, it's playtime!

Children build castles with glee and flair,
While snowball fights declare a fair share.
Siblings tumble in giggles galore,
Creating chaos, and wanting more!

A wise old owl with a frosty hat,
Comments on antics while watching the spat.
He chuckles softly with twinkling eyes,
At the winter antics beneath the skies.

So let the cold bring warmth to your soul,
In whispered memories, we all feel whole.
Gather around, share your laugh and cheer,
In this wonderful chill, love is near!

The Lurking Cold

Chill crept in like a sneaky cat,
Wearing mittens and a big top hat.
It whispered jokes in the frosty air,
While snowflakes giggled without a care.

The wind told tales of a winter feast,
Where snowmen danced and the hot cocoa ceased.
I tried to catch snowballs in my bare hands,
But they turned to ice, like my silly plans.

Penguins appeared, waddling with style,
They took my scarf and ran a wild mile.
Said they'd return it, but left me cold,
Those jokers made the best of the bold.

A snow plow honked like an angry bee,
While ice cubes skated around just for glee.
I laughed and shivered, all in good cheer,
In the lurking cold, I lost all fear.

Shadows of the Blizzard

In a swirling dance, the flakes took flight,
Dressed in white, feeling oh so bright.
They turned my dog into a fluffy clown,
As he tumbled and rolled all the way down.

The trees are giants, covered in white,
Their branches waving in a frosty fight.
Squirrels slipped, doing somersaults,
While my hot cocoa sloshed in small vaults.

The mailbox laughed with a friendly creak,
As I searched for letters, feeling quite weak.
Caught a snowball right in the face,
Guess winter's humor has its own grace.

It tickled my nose and made me shout,
I stood there laughing, frozen about.
In the midst of chaos, joy took its place,
In the blizzard's giggle, I found my space.

Frosted Whispers

A chill crept in, with a giggle and grin,
Said winter has come, let the fun begin.
Snowflakes fluttered like strange little fish,
As I made a wish for a warm marshmallow dish.

Trees were painting with frozen spritz,
Whispering secrets in frosty blitz.
A squirrel disputes, wearing a tiny hat,
I chuckled at him, 'That's quite a spat!'

Oh, how the ice decided to tease,
With slippery spots that brought me to knees.
Laughter erupted, for all it's worth,
Winter's crisp humor spread across the earth.

In every flake, a joke nicely spun,
Crafting a quilt of delightful fun.
Frosted whispers were all I could hear,
Making me chuckle, wiping a tear.

Shadows of Winter's Breath

Winter puffed out clouds, a magical sight,
Filled the air with giggles, pure delight.
Each breezy breath was a playful jest,
Chilling not just my cheeks, but my quest.

Gingerbread men danced on thawing ice,
With candy canes laughing, oh, so nice.
Snowballs flew with a comic's flare,
I ducked and dodged, but was caught unaware.

Puddles turned into frosty reflectors,
Creating laugh lines like comedy vectors.
In every step, a slip and a slide,
Winter's humor is hard to hide.

Toasting to life with cups held high,
While icicles giggle as they pass by.
With every breath, the joy was spread,
In the winter's laughter, I found my thread.

The Whisper of Falling Sparkles

A squirrel with boots, oh what a sight,
Sliding and gliding, in pure delight.
He giggles and twirls, on frosty ground,
Chasing his tail, round and round!

A snowman grins, with a carrot nose,
While a playful penguin strikes a pose.
They frolic and dance in a flurry of fun,
Making snow angels 'til the day is done.

Snowflakes tumble, a playful race,
Filling the air, brightening the space.
Winter's a stage, and laughter's the song,
Where silliness reigns and we all belong.

So let's join the parade, don't be shy,
Leave your worries, and let spirits fly.
In blankets of white, our joy takes flight,
With whispers of sparkles, the world feels right.

Forms of the Fleeting Cold

Look at the cat, with her frosty whiskers,
Pouncing on snowflakes, like little twisters.
She leaps and she bounds, her cheeks all aglow,
Even she wonders where those flakes go!

A snowball fight breaks out with glee,
As cold, wet projectiles fly rapidly.
Laughter erupts with each cheerful splat,
Who knew winter could make us so sprat?

Trees wear white caps, like grandpa's hat,
While ducks quack loudly, quite round and fat.
They waddle and quack, with style so bold,
In this chilly kingdom of forms untold.

So come, take a frolic, and join the crew,
With all of nature in a dazzling hue.
In the forms of the cold, let's dance and play,
Finding joy in the freeze of a winter's day.

The Wraiths Beneath the Blanket

Beneath the white, the creatures hide,
Bunnies and foxes, with fluff inside.
They peek and they dart, oh what a gig,
Playing hide and seek with a grand old fig!

The snow whispers secrets, over the ground,
As a lost mitten seeks where it's found.
A glove takes a leap, as if it can fly,
While the wind chortles, a mischievous sigh.

An elf with a snow shovel gets quite a shock,
Turns out it's a neighbor, not just a rock!
They both burst out laughing, despite the chill,
Making memories that winter can fill.

So gaze at the blanket, soft and wide,
For giggles and guffaws, there's truth inside.
In the wraiths we discover, with wonder unfurled,
There's humor and warmth in this frosty world.

The Chill of Hidden Stories

Old trees stand tall, with secrets to tell,
Of snowmen gone rogue, and a wintery spell.
They've seen playful hearts, and heard laughter soar,
In the chill of the days, they keep tales galore.

A snowflake slips, with a giggle so light,
"I bet you can't catch me, try as you might!"
They shimmy and swirl, with a twinkle and tease,
As winter unfolds her cool, gentle breeze.

Hot cocoa spills, with marshmallows bright,
As friends share their stories, in the soft night.
The hearth crackles softly, a symphony sweet,
While laughter wraps warmly, from head to feet.

So let's bundle up, as the tales unfold,
In the chill of the season, where memories mold.
Each tale brings a grin, and a giggle with ease,
In hidden stories, winter's gentle tease.

Traces on a Crystal Canvas

Tiny footsteps trace a line,
In sparkling white they intertwine.
A squirrel slips, a comical sight,
Lands in snow, oh what a fright!

A jolly snowman grins so wide,
With carrot nose and arms spread wide.
He tells jokes, they make us laugh,
While snowballs fly, it's a true gaffe!

The angels laugh from up above,
As we tumble in a snowy shove.
Laughter echoes through the air,
While fluffy flakes mess up our hair!

So when the winter's chill takes hold,
Embrace the fun, be brave, be bold.
For every trace we leave behind,
Is proof of joy, a life well-defined.

Phantoms on the Frost

A shadow peeks from behind the tree,
Is it a ghost? Or is it me?
A snowball fights a looming grin,
With frosty mitts, let's all dive in!

The frozen ground gives quite a crack,
As auntie slips, then tumbles back.
We giggle at her snow-filled hair,
While prancing 'round without a care.

The owls hoot in their icy thrones,
We're here on earth, where humor roams.
We dance like phantoms, swirling about,
In a winter wonder where laughter's loud.

With every spark of white that falls,
We build a fort with snowy walls.
So let's not fret, embrace the chill,
For in this fun, there's surely a thrill!

Ethereal Dance of the Elements

A snowflake swirls, like a gentle whiff,
Tickles my nose, a light-hearted gift.
Frosted whispers through trees do sway,
As winter's breath plays hide and say!

Softly, whispers turn into cheers,
While children giggle, abandoning fears.
An icy slide without a doubt,
A bumpy ride - who's laughing now?

The wind tosses hats, it's quite the sport,
As everyone scrambles to retake their court.
A gentle tug pulls at the fun,
As laughter glows beneath the sun.

Let's conjure magic in this cold,
While weaving tales, bright and bold.
With elements playing, we twist and twine,
In a frosty dance, it's purely divine!

Silence Wrapped in White

A silent white, a world anew,
Wrapped in laughter, yes, that's our cue.
The dogs dash by, a rush of fur,
While flurries whirl, in a soft purr.

Snow piles high on a beaming face,
With giggles ringing, we race, we chase.
The snowman winks – what a good chap!
While we conspire to cover him with a cap!

Lurking snowflakes just won't land,
As we throw our boots in a wonderland.
With every step, a funny fall,
Into the fluff – we're having a ball!

In this quiet world, let's be carefree,
With giggles echoing, wild with glee.
For every snowflake's frosty embrace,
Brings laughter to this snowy space.

Milton Keynes UK
Ingram Content Group UK Ltd.
UKHW021021251124
451242UK00021B/76